Dog

CW00867145

Facts for Fun!

Book B

By Wyatt Michaels

Copyright 2012

All rights reserved.

No duplication without the express
written permission of the author.

Images courtesy of Camry Ruth Ellison, Wedding Photography by Jon Day, and Mythic Sea Bass

What breed was the seventh most popular breed in 2011?

A. Beagle
B. Bichon Frise
C. Boxer

Image courtesy of wilybo

The answer is C. Boxer

They ranked higher in 2009 as sixth most popular breed. Beagles ranked higher yet in 4th place.

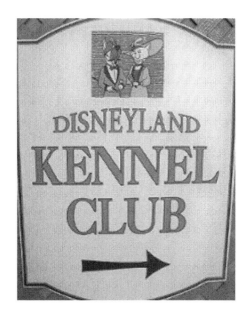

Image courtesy of Loren Javier

Which breed is not considered to be a terrier by the American Kennel Club?

A. Bull Terrier
B. Border Terrier
C. Boston Terrier

Image courtesy of swambo

The answer is C. Boston Terrier

These dogs aren't terriers, but they were the first U.S. breed to be recognized by the American Kennel Club.

Image courtesy of Sister72

Which breed used to accompany organ grinders and do tricks in circuses and fairs?

A. Bichon Frise

B. Bull Terrier

C. Boxer

Image courtesy of swaggyp

The answer is A. Bichon Frise

Years before that, they were popular in the paintings of many Spanish artists.

Image courtesy of public domain

Which breed is the mascot for Boston University in Massachusetts and Wofford College in South Carolina?

A. Boxer
B. Boston Terrier
C. Bull Terrier

Image courtesy of public domain

The answer is B. Boston Terrier

These schools have chosen a dog known as the "American Gentleman" for their mascot.

Images courtesy of Llima and Lilly M.

The nickname for which breed is "barkless dog".

A. Basenji
B. Bull Terrier
C. Basset Hound

Image courtesy of lindyi

The answer is A. Basenji

Instead of barking, their yodel-like sound is called a "barroo".

Image courtesy of Vicky Frank

Also testing your knowledge of the classics, what breed was Lassie's friend, Pokey, from early in the Lassie TV series?

A. Basset Hound
B. Beagle
C. Bichon Frise

Image courtesy of donjd2

The answer is A. Basset Hound

Also, a basset hound kept a lonely Maytag Man company in Maytag advertisements, and a basset hound named Lafayette was in the Disney movie, Aristocats.

Image courtesy of lednichenkoolga

Which breed is used to detect termites in Australia?

A. Border Collie
B. Basset Hound
C. Beagle

Image courtesy of mcn2zst

The answer is C. Beagle

Although they were originally bred for hunting, Beagles are also used in pet therapy in hospitals, and detection of drugs and explosives.

Image courtesy of public domain

Bandit, Laura's second dog on Little House on the Prairie, was one of these.

A. Border Collie
B. Beagle
C. Boston Terrier

Image courtesy of Robb

The answer is A. Border Collie

Bandit replaced Laura's beloved dog,
Jack. He premiered in the second
season of the show, and continued to be
on it for the next three years.

Images courtesy of public domain, Mythic Seas Bass, and Lilly M.

Which breed has a large egg-shaped head and triangular eyes?

A. Boxer
B. Basenji
C. Bull Terrier

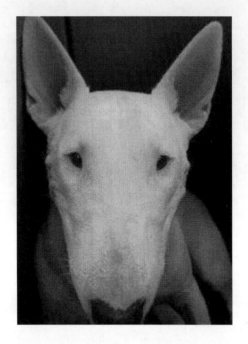

Image courtesy of Behemot

The answer is C. Bull Terrier

It also has a jaunty gait and is popularly known as the "gladiator of the canine race".

Image courtesy of iconoclast

Which breed is considered to be the most intelligent?

A. Bull Terrier
B. Border Collie
C. Beagle

Image courtesy of Dave-F

The answer is B. Border Collie

Border Collies also excel in agility competitions that include flyball, tracking, and sheepdog trials.

Image courtesy of andertoons

Which breed's most famous dog appears in a comic strip?

A. Beagle
B. Basset Hound
C. Bull Terrier

Image courtesy of cristianocani

The answer is A. Beagle

Snoopy is considered the "world's most famous Beagle".

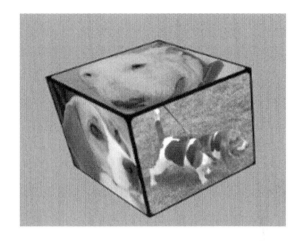

Images courtesy of soundfromwayout, Lilly M., and Camry Ruth Ellison

Famous dogs in this breed include Spuds McKenzie and Bullseye.

A. Bull Terrier
B. Basset Hound
C. Beagle

Image courtesy of Pleple2000

The answer is A. Bull Terrier

Bud Light featured Spuds McKenzie in the late 1980's. Bullseye is the trademark for Target stores.

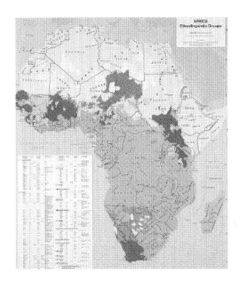

Image courtesy of Norman B. Leventhal Map
Center at the BPL

Which breed originated in Africa and is possibly one of the earliest known breeds?

A. Boxer

B. Basenji

C. Basset Hound

Image courtesy of Sannse

The answer is B. Basenji

Pictures of Basenji-like dogs can be seen in the slabs of the tombs of Egyptian pharaohs.

Image courtesy of vrt3

Which breed has a dog named Jason that is in the logo for Hush Puppies brand of shoes?

A. Bichon Frise
B. Basset Hound
C. Boston Terrier

Image courtesy of public domain

The answer is B. Basset Hound

The Basset Hound is Hush Puppies first and only logo since 1958.

Image courtesy of ndanger

Which breed was used by the military in WWI (and since) as messenger dogs and pack carriers?

A. Boxer
B. Border Collie
C. Basset Hound

Image courtesy of Peter Hellberg

The answer is A. Boxer

Boxers were used as attack and guard dogs during the war as well. After the war, they became pets and show dogs.

Image courtesy of Ariaski

Which breed is used to lead blind people?

   A. Bichon Frise
   B. Border Collie
   C. Basset Hound

Image courtesy of public domain

The answer is A. Bichon Frise

This was during the late 1800's. Bichon Frises have also been companion dogs for sailors.

Image courtesy of Alexandre Dulaunoy

Which breed is especially good at
herding sheep?

A. Beagle
B. Basenji
C. Border Collie

Image courtesy of Puppies are Prozac

The answer is C. Border Collie

They take direction by voice or whistle from a long distance. They are also used to remove unwanted birds from airport runways and golf courses.

Image courtesy of public domain

Which breed originated in France and was bred to hunt rabbits?

A. Beagle
B. Basset Hound
C. Boxer

Image courtesy of public domain

The answer is B. Basset Hound

The white tip on their tail is said to help hunters find the dog when they are tracking through underbrush.

Image courtesy of shutterhacks

The title character for the 1954 novel and 1956 movie "Good-bye, My Lady" was which breed?

A. Boston Terrier
B. Border Collie
C. Basenji

Image courtesy of public domain

The answer is C. Basenji

The cast of the movie included Walter Brennan and Sidney Poitier.

Images courtesy of Camry Ruth Ellison, Lilly M.
and Puppies are Prozac

Which breed ranks first out of all dog
breeds in pound-for-pound muscle
tissue?

A. Beagle
B. Bull Terrier
C. Border Collie

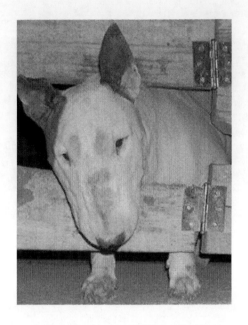

Image courtesy of katesheets

The answer is B. Bull Terrier

It is said they don't seek to start a fight,
but they are very good at finishing one.

Image courtesy of Grace Family

Two dogs of which breed were named Rex and Fly in the 1995 movie "Babe"?

A. Bull Terrier
B. Beagle
C. Border Collie

Image courtesy of Tambako the Jaguar

The answer is C. Border Collie

They also appeared in the sequel Babe: Pig in the City.

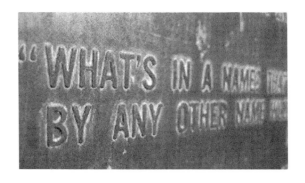

Image courtesy of jack Dorsey

The name of which breed means "curly lap dog"?

A. Basenji

B. Boston Terrier

C. Bichon Frise

Image courtesy of mrRobot

The answer is C. Bichon Frise

The dogs originated in Spain or Belgium but the name is French.

Images courtesy of public domain,
soundfromwayout, and Camry Ruth Ellison

Which breed's ears are so long that
puppies easily trip over their own?

A. Basset Hound
B. Beagle
C. Basenji

Image courtesy of Marilyn Jane

The answer is A. Basset Hound

They may be short, but because their
bodies are so long, they can reach things
on table tops that may surprise you.

Image courtesy of Horia Varlan

What kind of dog has been known to learn and respond to over 1,000 words?

A. Basenji

B. Border Collie

C. Boxer

Image courtesy of public domain

The answer is B. Border Collie

In 2010, a Border Collie named Chaser had a vocabulary of 1022 words.

Image courtesy of Greg Walters

Which breed was originally bred to hunt rats in garment factories?

A. Boston Terrier
B. Beagle
C. Boxer

Image courtesy of A. Blight

The answer is A. Boston Terrier

They are now bred to be companion
dogs. They tend to have a quiet,
friendly and happy-go-lucky
personality.

Image courtesy of MiK

Which breed appears in the movies, Underdog, Cats & Dogs, Shiloh, and The Wonder Years?

A. Boxer
B. Bichon Frise
C. Beagle

Image courtesy of darkripper

The answer is C. Beagle

Gromit in the film series, Wallace and Gromit, is also a Beagle.

Congratulations! You can now impress your family and friends with what you know about dog breeds that start with "b".

Look for more quiz books by Wyatt Michaels about other dog breeds, baseball, letter sounds, careers, football, horses, presidents, states, and more.

17720297R00032

Printed in Great Britain
by Amazon